Bach

Sonata No. 1 in B minor

Kuhlau

Duet No. 1 in E minor, Op. 10
Duet No. 2 in D major

3344

MMO CD 3344

Music Minus One

BACH: Sonata No. 1 in B minor

DISC A

DISC B

Printed in Canada

SONATA NO. 1 in B MINOR

FLUTE

4 beats (1 measure) precede music.

ANDANTE

J.S. BACH

MMOCD 3344

4

6

MMOCD 3344

7

8

ALLEGRO MODERATO

DUET NO. 1 in E MINOR

1st FLUTE

KUHLAU

3 beats (1 measure) precede music.
ALLEGRO CON ESPRESSIONE

6 loud / 3 soft beats precede entrance
of 2nd flute. Start on 1st soft beat.
LARGHETTO

1st FLUTE

14

1st FLUTE

DUET NO. 2 in D MAJOR

KUHLAU

2 beats (1 measure) precede music.
ALLEGRISSIMO

16

4 beats (1measure) precede music.
RONDO

MMO Compact Disc Catalog

BROADWAY

CLARINET

PIANO

PIANO - FOUR HANDS

VIOLIN

MMO Music Group, 50 Executive Boulevard, Elmsford, New York 10523, 1 (800) 669-7464

MMO Compact Disc Catalog

HAYDN String Quartet Op. 76 No. 6 .... MMO CD 3136
BEAUTIFUL MUSIC FOR TWO VIOLINS 1st position, vol. 1 .... MMO CD 3137 *
BEAUTIFUL MUSIC FOR TWO VIOLINS 2nd position, vol. 2 .... MMO CD 3138 *
BEAUTIFUL MUSIC FOR TWO VIOLINS 3rd position, vol. 3 .... MMO CD 3139 *
BEAUTIFUL MUSIC FOR TWO VIOLINS 1st, 2nd, 3rd position, vol. 4 .... MMO CD 3140 *
TEACHER'S PARTNER Basic Violin Studies 1st year .... MMO CD 3142
DVORAK STRING TRIO "Terzetto", OP. 74 2 violins/viola .... MMO CD 3143
SIBELIUS VIOLIN Concerto in D Minor, OPUS 47 .... MMO CD 3144

*Lovely folk tunes and selections from the classics, chosen for their melodic beauty and technical value. They have been skillfully transcribed and edited by Samuel Applebaum, one of America's foremost teachers.

GUITAR

BOCCHERINI Quintet No. 4 in D "Fandango" .... MMO CD 3601
GIULIANI Quintet in A Op. 65 .... MMO CD 3602
CLASSICAL GUITAR DUETS .... MMO CD 3603
RENAISSANCE & BAROQUE GUITAR DUETS .... MMO CD 3604
CLASSICAL & ROMANTIC GUITAR DUETS .... MMO CD 3605
GUITAR AND FLUTE DUETS Volume 1 .... MMO CD 3606
GUITAR AND FLUTE DUETS Volume 2 .... MMO CD 3607
BLUEGRASS GUITAR .... MMO CD 3608
GEORGE BARNES GUITAR METHOD Lessons from a Master .... MMO CD 3609
HOW TO PLAY FOLK GUITAR 2 CD Set .... MMO CD 3610
FAVORITE FOLKS SONGS FOR GUITAR .... MMO CD 3611
FOR GUITARS ONLY! Jimmy Raney Small Band Arrangements .... MMO CD 3612
TEN DUETS FOR TWO GUITARS Geo. Barnes/Carl Kress .... MMO CD 3613
PLAY THE BLUES GUITAR A Dick Weissman Method .... MMO CD 3614
ORCHESTRAL GEMS FOR CLASSICAL GUITAR .... MMO CD 3615

FLUTE

MOZART Concerto No. 2 in D, QUANTZ Concerto in G .... MMO CD 3300
MOZART Concerto in G K.313 .... MMO CD 3301
BACH Suite No. 2 in B Minor .... MMO CD 3302
BOCCHERINI Concerto in D, VIVALDI Concerto in G Minor "La Notte",
MOZART Andante for Strings .... MMO CD 3303
HAYDN Divertimento, VIVALDI Concerto in D Op. 10 No. 3 "Bullfinch",
FREDERICK THE GREAT Concerto in C .... MMO CD 3304
VIVALDI Conc. in F; TELEMANN Conc. in D; LECLAIR Conc. in C .... MMO CD 3305
BACH Brandenburg No. 2 in F, HAYDN Concerto in D .... MMO CD 3306
BACH Triple Concerto, VIVALDI Concerto in D Minor .... MMO CD 3307
MOZART Quartet in F, STAMITZ Quartet in F .... MMO CD 3308
HAYDN 4 London Trios for 2 Flutes & Cello .... MMO CD 3309
BACH Brandenburg Concerti Nos. 4 & 5 .... MMO CD 3310
MOZART 3 Flute Quartets in D, A and C .... MMO CD 3311
TELEMANN Suite in A Minor, GLUCK Scene from 'Orpheus',
PERGOLESI Concerto in G (2 CD Set) .... MMO CD 3312
FLUTE SONG: Easy Familiar Classics .... MMO CD 3313
VIVALDI Concerti In D, G, and F .... MMO CD 3314
VIVALDI Concerti in A Minor, G, and D .... MMO CD 3315
EASY FLUTE SOLOS Beginning Students Volume 1 .... MMO CD 3316
EASY FLUTE SOLOS Beginning Students Volume 2 .... MMO CD 3317
EASY JAZZ DUETS Student Level .... MMO CD 3318
FLUTE & GUITAR DUETS Volume 1 .... MMO CD 3319
FLUTE & GUITAR DUETS Volume 2 .... MMO CD 3320
BEGINNING CONTEST SOLOS Murray Panitz .... MMO CD 3321
BEGINNING CONTEST SOLOS Donald Peck .... MMO CD 3322
INTERMEDIATE CONTEST SOLOS Julius Baker .... MMO CD 3323
INTERMEDIATE CONTEST SOLOS Donald Peck .... MMO CD 3324
ADVANCED CONTEST SOLOS Murray Panitz .... MMO CD 3325
ADVANCED CONTEST SOLOS Julius Baker .... MMO CD 3326
INTERMEDIATE CONTEST SOLOS Donald Peck .... MMO CD 3327
ADVANCED CONTEST SOLOS Murray Panitz .... MMO CD 3328
ADVANCED CONTEST SOLOS Julius Baker .... MMO CD 3329
BEGINNING CONTEST SOLOS Doriot Anthony Dwyer .... MMO CD 3330
INTERMEDIATE CONTEST SOLOS Doriot Anthony Dwyer .... MMO CD 3331
ADVANCED CONTEST SOLOS Doriot Anthony Dwyer .... MMO CD 3332
FIRST CHAIR SOLOS with Orchestral Accompaniment .... MMO CD 3333
TEACHER'S PARTNER Basic Flute Studies 1st year .... MMO CD 3334
THE JOY OF WOODWIND MUSIC .... MMO CD 3335
JEWELS FOR WOODWIND QUINTET .... MMO CD 3336
BOLLING: SUITE FOR FLUTE/JAZZ PIANO TRIO .... MMO CD 3342
HANDEL / TELEMANN SIX SONATAS 2 CD Set .... MMO CD 3343
BACH SONATA NO. 1 in Bm / KUHLAU TWO DUETS in Em/D MAJOR 2 CD Set .... MMO CD 3344
KUHLAU TRIO for 3 FLUTES IN Eb, OP. 86 / BACH 2 SONATAS IN Eb/A 2 CD Set .... MMO CD 3345
PEPUSCH SONATA IN C / TELEMANN SONATA IN Cm .... MMO CD 3346
QUANTZ TRIO SONATA IN Cm / BACH GIGUE / ABEL SON. 2 IN F .... MMO CD 3347
TELEMANN CONCERTO NO. 1 IN D / CORRETTE SONATA IN E MINOR .... MMO CD 3348
TELEMANN TRIO IN F / Bb MAJOR / HANDEL SON. #3 IN C MAJOR .... MMO CD 3349
MARCELLO / TELEMANN / HANDEL SONATAS IN F MAJOR .... MMO CD 3350
CONCERT BAND FAVORITES WITH ORCHESTRA .... MMO CD 3351
BAND-AIDS CONCERT BAND FAVORITES WITH ORCHESTRA .... MMO CD 3352

RECORDER

PLAYING THE RECORDER Folk Songs of Many Naitons .... MMO CD 3337
LET'S PLAY THE RECORDER Beginning Children's Method .... MMO CD 3338
YOU CAN PLAY THE RECORDER Beginning Adult Method .... MMO CD 3339
3 SONATAS FOR FLUTE, HARPSICHORD & VIOLA DA GAMBA .... MMO CD 3340
3 SONATAS FOR ALTO RECORDER .... MMO CD 3341

FRENCH HORN

MOZART Concerti No. 2 & No. 3 in Eb. K. 417 & 447 .... MMO CD 3501
BAROQUE BRASS AND BEYOND .... MMO CD 3502
MUSIC FOR BRASS ENSEMBLE .... MMO CD 3503
MOZART Sonatas for Two Horns .... MMO CD 3504
BEGINNING CONTEST SOLOS Mason Jones .... MMO CD 3511
BEGINNING CONTEST SOLOS Myron Bloom .... MMO CD 3512
INTERMEDIATE CONTEST SOLOS Dale Clevenger .... MMO CD 3513
INTERMEDIATE CONTEST SOLOS Mason Jones .... MMO CD 3514
ADVANCED CONTEST SOLOS Myron Bloom .... MMO CD 3515
ADVANCED CONTEST SOLOS Dale Clevenger .... MMO CD 3516
INTERMEDIATE CONTEST SOLOS Mason Jones .... MMO CD 3517
ADVANCED CONTEST SOLOS Myron Bloom .... MMO CD 3518
INTERMEDIATE CONTEST SOLOS Dale Clevenger .... MMO CD 3519
FRENCH HORN WOODWIND MUSIC .... MMO CD 3520
MASTERPIECES FOR WOODWIND QUINTET .... MMO CD 3521
FRENCH HORN UP FRONT BRASS QUINTETS .... MMO CD 3522
HORN OF PLENTY BRASS QUINTETS .... MMO CD 3523
BAND-AIDS CONCERT BAND FAVORITES WITH ORCHESTRA .... MMO CD 3524

TRUMPET

THREE CONCERTI: HAYDN, TELEMANN, FASCH .... MMO CD 3801
TRUMPET SOLOS Student Level Volume 1 .... MMO CD 3802
TRUMPET SOLOS Student Level Volume 2 .... MMO CD 3803
EASY JAZZ DUETS Student Level .... MMO CD 3804
MUSIC FOR BRASS ENSEMBLE Brass Quintets .... MMO CD 3805
FIRST CHAIR TRUMPET SOLOS with Orchestral Accompaniment .... MMO CD 3806
THE ART OF THE SOLO TRUMPET with Orchestral Accompaniment .... MMO CD 3807
BAROQUE BRASS AND BEYOND Brass Quintets .... MMO CD 3808
THE COMPLETE ARBAN DUETS all of the classic studies .... MMO CD 3809
SOUSA MARCHES PLUS BEETHOVEN, BERLIOZ, STRAUSS .... MMO CD 3810
BEGINNING CONTEST SOLOS Gerard Schwarz .... MMO CD 3811
BEGINNING CONTEST SOLOS Armando Ghitalla .... MMO CD 3812
INTERMEDIATE CONTEST SOLOS Robert Nagel, Soloist .... MMO CD 3813
INTERMEDIATE CONTEST SOLOS Gerard Schwarz .... MMO CD 3814
ADVANCED CONTEST SOLOS Robert Nagel, Soloist .... MMO CD 3815
CONTEST SOLOS Armando Ghitalla .... MMO CD 3816
INTERMEDIATE CONTEST SOLOS Gerard Schwarz .... MMO CD 3817
ADVANCED CONTEST SOLOS Robert Nagel, Soloist .... MMO CD 3818
ADVANCED CONTEST SOLOS Armando Ghilalla .... MMO CD 3819
BEGINNING CONTEST SOLOS Raymond Crisara .... MMO CD 3820
BEGINNING CONTEST SOLOS Raymond Crisara .... MMO CD 3821
INTERMEDIATE CONTEST SOLOS Raymond Crisara .... MMO CD 3822
TEACHER'S PARTNER Basic Trumpet Studies 1st year .... MMO CD 3823
TWENTY DIXIELAND CLASSICS .... MMO CD 3824
TWENTY RHYTHM BACKGROUNDS TO STANDARDS .... MMO CD 3825
FROM DIXIE TO SWING .... MMO CD 3826
TRUMPET PIECES BRASS QUINTETS .... MMO CD 3827
MODERN BRASS QUINTETS .... MMO CD 3828
WHEN JAZZ WAS YOUNG The Bob Wilber All Stars .... MMO CD 3829
CONCERT BAND FAVORITES WITH ORCHESTRA .... MMO CD 3831
BAND-AIDS CONCERT BAND FAVORITES WITH ORCHESTRA .... MMO CD 3832

TROMBONE

TROMBONE SOLOS Student Level Volume 1 .... MMO CD 3901
TROMBONE SOLOS Student Level Volume 2 .... MMO CD 3902
EASY JAZZ DUETS Student Level .... MMO CD 3903
BAROQUE BRASS & BEYOND Brass Quintets .... MMO CD 3904
MUSIC FOR BRASS ENSEMBLE Brass Quintets .... MMO CD 3905
BEGINNING CONTEST SOLOS Per Brevig .... MMO CD 3911
BEGINNING CONTEST SOLOS Jay Friedman .... MMO CD 3912
INTERMEDIATE CONTEST SOLOS Keith Brown, Professor, Indiana University .... MMO CD 3913
INTERMEDIATE CONTEST SOLOS Jay Friedman .... MMO CD 3914
ADVANCED CONTEST SOLOS Keith Brown, Professor, Indiana University .... MMO CD 3915
ADVANCED CONTEST SOLOS Per Brevig .... MMO CD 3916
ADVANCED CONTEST SOLOS Keith Brown, Professor, Indiana University .... MMO CD 3917
ADVANCED CONTEST SOLOS Jay Friedman .... MMO CD 3918
ADVANCED CONTEST SOLOS Per Brevig .... MMO CD 3919
TEACHER'S PARTNER Basic Trombone Studies 1st year .... MMO CD 3920
TWENTY DIXIELAND CLASSICS .... MMO CD 3924
TWENTY RHYTHM BACKGROUNDS TO STANDARDS .... MMO CD 3925
FROM DIXIE TO SWING .... MMO CD 3926
STICKS & BONES BRASS QUINTETS .... MMO CD 3927
FOR TROMBONES ONLY MORE BRASS QUINTETS .... MMO CD 3928
POPULAR CONCERT FAVORITES The Stuttgart Festival Band .... MMO CD 3929
BAND-AIDS CONCERT BAND FAVORITES WITH ORCHESTRA .... MMO CD 3930

MMO Music Group, 50 Executive Boulevard, Elmsford, New York 10523, 1 (800) 669-7464

Bach

Sonata No. 1 in B minor

Kuhlau

Duet No. 1 in E minor, Op. 10
Duet No. 2 in D major

3344

MMO Music Group, 50 Executive Boulevard, Elmsford, New York 10523, 1 (800) 669-7464